Home Buyer Secrets

DANIEL JAMES LESNIAK & KERI SHULL

Daniel James Lesniak and Keri Shull Home Buyer Secrets

Published by: DKB Publishing

Text Design by: Marcia Eppich-Harris

A CIP record for this book is available from the Library of Congress Cataloging-in-Publication Data.

ISBN-13: 978-0-9983545-3-8

Contents

Introduction

Thank you for reading *Home Buyer Secrets*.

Our real estate team—The Keri Shull and Orange Line Living Team—is a perennial top team in the country, as ranked by REAL Trends in *The Wall Street Journal*. In addition to helping hundreds of home buyers every year, Keri and I have bought, invested, planned, and helped develop over 350 homes ourselves.

In total, Keri and I have helped thousands of buyers and sold over $2 billion worth of real estate. All that experience has given us unique perspectives on home buying and home-ownership.

Buying a home is one of the surest paths to building wealth—but **only when you buy your home correctly.**

Every year our team helps several hundred buyers and sellers. No two real estate transactions are ever exactly alike, but we do see certain potential issues come up routinely.

What we have found from helping thousands of people is that **most home buying problems can be prevented** through up-front education. This education is also the surest way to save money when buying your home. But the information that will save you the most money and reduce the time you spend on the home buying process is hard to come by.

Too many home buyers get inaccurate or incomplete information. Whether it is because real estate agents do not take the time to educate their clients or because those agents are stuck in an old-school mentality, most buyers are left in the dark about the best ways to save time and money—and to prevent stress—when buying a home.

In the sections that follow we'll talk first about how homeownership builds wealth. Then we'll deal with the question of whether buying a home makes sense for you. Once we've settled that question, we'll learn about ways to finance a home; search for homes that meet your price range and needs; write the offer and negotiate for the best possible price; and close the deal. We'll also talk about how to build a team that will save you time, save you money, and protect you from costly mistakes as well as stress.

What I have learned by operating several successful businesses and investing millions of dollars in real estate is that executing quickly is what separates those who enjoy success and those who fall short. In a seller's market, **speed is essential to winning the property you want**. Even in a buyer's market, **speed can help you get the best possible deal**. But in order to execute quickly and save more money, you need accurate information about the latest and most effective methods and strategies. That's where the traditional professional real estate industry falls short.

Our goal is to prepare you early in the home buying process so that you're equipped with all the information you need to make important decisions without feeling rushed. Inside this book you'll find our team's best secrets to help you save time, reduce stress, make informed decisions, and get the best possible deal on your best possible home.

Before we explain the home buying process, Keri and I want to share our story so you know who we are and what qualifies us to guide you on this life-changing journey.

Our story

Prior to starting our careers in real estate, Keri and I both moved a lot.

Keri's family *moved over 15 times* during her childhood, following her dad's career wherever it led.

Inspired by both the good and bad experiences her family had while relocating, Keri graduated from Penn State and began selling new homes, first for NVHomes and then for the Mayhood Company. Between 2003 and 2008 she became one of the highest-selling salespersons for new communities and condo buildings. During this time Keri often invested in homes herself and succeeded with both flipping and buy-and-hold strategies.

Within five years of graduating college, Keri had built a multi-million-dollar real estate portfolio with multiple cash-flowing properties.

In 2008, Keri left the new home sales industry and became a real estate agent to help people buy and sell all types of homes. She had immediate success, began building a team, and quickly became the top agent at her RE/MAX office. She later left RE/MAX and moved her team to Keller Williams, became the top agent at that office, and within a few years became one of the top four agents in the world at Keller Williams.

Like Keri, I moved a lot—though for different reasons. After leaving my home for the Naval Academy, I moved over nine times during the next 10 years in the Navy. Because I was in the Navy, I had access to no-money-down Veterans Affairs (VA) loans and bought my first home at the age of 23.

Over the next nine years, I did just about everything you can do as a residential real estate investor: I bought homes, became a landlord, sold some of those homes, and made money on all but one of my deals. I experienced one of the greatest real estate markets, one of the biggest falls, and the subsequent recovery. Before ever going into real estate as a profession, I built up a multimillion-dollar real estate portfolio without ever earning more than $100,000 from work.

After my career as a submarine officer in the Navy and a defense contractor, I began my real estate career in 2012.

When I graduated from Georgetown's MBA program, I did not expect to go into real estate as a career, but I got my license while I was buying my second home in the area. My goal after leaving business school was to make a jump up the corporate ladder and get a position at a strategy consulting firm. After being told by several interviewers at some of the biggest strategy consulting firms that I did not have the sales acumen required for the position, I decided to quit my contracting job and become a full-time real estate agent.

I implemented an innovative strategy informed by my unique education and experience. I immediately became the top agent at my Century 21 office—and one of the top agents in my entire market. I sold over $22 million in real estate during my first year, and this later became the basis for my best-selling book, *The HyperLocal HyperFast Real Estate Agent*, which has helped thousands of real estate agents nationwide.

Keri and I first met in 2013 when I moved to the Keller Williams office where she worked. While I recruited her to join my new title company, we made an instant connection. We became close friends, then dated, and after a short while decided to get married and merge our businesses. Before we left to start our own brokerage, we built our Keller Williams team to one of the top four teams in the world.

In 2015, the first full year of our new brokerage, we helped over 360 people buy or sell a home, becoming the number one team in Virginia and one of the top 40 teams in the entire nation. In 2018 we helped nearly 500 buyers and sellers, and sold over $300 million in real estate.

The reason I tell you all of this is because I want you to understand that our advice comes from our actual experience and success.

That brings us to an important point.

Be careful where you get your advice

Although the Information Age we live in has many benefits, one of the drawbacks is that **it is too easy for unqualified people to pose as "experts"** and give out advice in areas they have little actual experience in— or even give advice on things they have never done themselves.

This book is designed to help you with one of the largest financial decisions you will ever make, and I want you to know you are getting your real estate advice from people who are qualified to give it.

Keri and I have helped thousands of buyers and sellers and sold over $2 billion in real estate. We have been investors, developers, and syndicators for over 350 new homes. We have been investors or partners in several joint ventures and technology start-ups related to real estate. We've had success at every part of the home development and sales process—giving us unique insight into the home buying process.

I am not telling you all of this to brag. I'm telling you because we want you to confidently know that the advice in this book comes from following the process hundreds of times for ourselves and *thousands* of times for others. We've even trained thousands of other real estate agents nationwide—and now we want to bring that knowledge to as many home buyers as we can.

Since we are constantly seeing new developments in the market, we have put together a resource page where you can see the latest home buyer secrets we are using to help our clients save time and money. To access these materials, go to thehomebuyersecrets.com.

How homeownership creates wealth

Owning real estate has been one of the most reliable ways to create and preserve wealth for centuries. According to McKinney Capital & Advisory,1over 90% of today's millionaires built their wealth through real estate—not through stocks, start-up investments, or starting a business.

Real estate may not seem as sexy as entrepreneurial ventures or hot start-up investments, but real estate has historically been the reliable workhorse for building wealth.

I know a lot of wealthy people, and the one thing they have in common is that they own real estate. Usually when I ask them if they have any regrets about owning real estate, their answer is only that they wish they had started sooner.

Owning a home builds wealth in four primary ways: **Leveraged Appreciation**, **Principal Paydown**, **Tax Breaks**, and **Locking in Housing Costs**.

1. **Leveraged Appreciation** – Most people buy their homes with very favorable loans. The loans are usually 80% of the purchase price, but sometimes even more. Options exist for financing 95% of a

---

1 http://www.mckinneycapital.com/90-percent-of-millionaires-do-this/.

home and even up to 100% when buying. Since the early 2000s, mortgage rates have dropped to historical lows in the United States. Getting to borrow so much money at such a low rate is simply unheard-of with other types of investments. For example, if you are buying stocks on the margin, it is usually impossible to borrow more than 50%. Getting to borrow so much provides a huge advantage in real estate. You get to keep 100% of the appreciation even though you only came up with funds for a much smaller percentage. For example, if you put down 20% of the purchase price, and the home goes up 10% of the value, the return on your initial investment is five times 10% or a whopping 50%. This is because you get to take advantage of a 5x leverage. See the chart below for more examples.

LEGEND
- YOUR INVESTMENT
- YOUR LOAN FROM THE BANK
- YOUR PROFIT

2. **Principal Paydown** – If you own a home and pay a mortgage, every time you make a payment you're paying down the balance. That is building up equity and putting money in your own pocket. If you are renting, all that money is going straight to your landlord's pocket. If your mortgage is $2,000 a month, in the first few years of the loan approximately $500 a month is going toward your principal. This will vary depending on interest rate, the type of loan, and what stage of the loan you are in, but this number is a good rule of thumb. As you can see, this will add up over time. In a year, just by paying your mortgage, you will have saved $6,000 through reducing the balance of your loan. In five years it would be over $30,000. So another way that owning your own home builds wealth is that it creates a kind of automatic monthly savings program.

3. **Tax Breaks** – Homeowners get tax advantages that renters do not. Depending on the state you live in and your financial picture, the tax advantages of owning your own home will vary. Recent tax law changes have impacted real estate tax deductions for many people, but it is still worth analyzing tax effects when considering a home. The interest on mortgages is tax-deductible up to a balance of $750,000. If your mortgage is above $750,000, you still get the deduction up to the $750,000 mark. Property taxes, which are included in most people's

mortgage payment, are also tax-deductible. There is a $10,000 annual limit in the deductions from state and local taxes, but most homeowners will fall under this limit. The other item to consider when analyzing the tax effects of owning a home is how your itemized deductions compare to the standard deduction. The new tax law has increased the standard deduction to $12,000, $18,000, and $24,000 depending on whether you file as single, married, or married filing separately. The combination of these new changes will reduce the tax benefits of the mortgage interest deduction, and for many people the standard deduction will be higher. Buyers in higher price point areas with higher incomes will stand to benefit more. When you are deciding whether it makes sense for you to buy a home, you need to look at whether the mortgage deduction will benefit you—and by how much.

4. **Locking in Housing Costs** – Most renters face yearly rent hikes of 2–3%. If you own your home, most of the costs are fixed. Yes, taxes can go up, as well as insurance and other costs, but most of the payment remains the same. This is true for fixed rate mortgages and adjustable rate mortgages (ARMs) during their initial fixed period. If you are renting and face a 3% annual rent increase, by the fifth year you will be paying 15% more than the first year. By the tenth year, you would be paying a 34% increase. Over time, the financial benefits of locking in your cost of living really add up.

As you can see, real estate provides several advantages that increase your overall net worth—and usually these advantages compound over time.

In additional to the financial benefits of homeownership, many homeowners would say that owning a home gives them feelings of **security, consistency, pride,** and **connection to the community.**

Step 1

Decide whether to buy or rent

Despite the many benefits of homeownership, buying a home is not for everyone. Here are some initial questions I believe you should ask yourself when you start thinking about buying a home.

How long do you think you will live in the area?

If you know you are very likely to stay in an area for at least two or three years, this will almost always make it a good idea to buy a home.

Real estate offers many benefits, but it does rack up more transaction costs than many other investments—usually around 7% when you add up the costs of selling, transaction taxes, and other costs. So if you are going to sell a property, it might take you two or three years of price appreciation at 2–3% a year to overcome the transaction costs.

Even if you plan to live in an area for less than three years, owning could still be beneficial. If you are open to the possibility of being a landlord, you can benefit from even more tax advantages by having someone else pay you rent and getting depreciation credits.

I have purchased several homes that I lived in for three years or less. In some cases, I rented the home to tenants after moving out. In other cases, I sold the home for a profit.

Many people think that buying a home gives them less flexibility than renting, but I have found that owning a home gives you *more* flexibility.

How does renting in your area compare to owning?

Before deciding to buy, compare the costs of owning a home to the costs of renting. This will vary by city and will be influenced by factors that include, but are not limited to, the following:

- Home prices in the area
- Total housing inventory
- Expected housing appreciation
- Rent costs in the area
- Total rental inventory
- Expected rent inflation
- Local job market and economy

Just because an area has high home prices does not mean renting is a better option. In fact, if the costs of renting are even higher, it might be more affordable to buy a high-priced home than when comparing to much lower-priced areas. Likewise, an area with lower-priced homes could be a better place to rent your home if the rental prices are lower as a percentage of the cost to buy.

What do your financial savings look like?

Even if buying makes more long-term sense than renting, you need to make sure that buying a home will not put you in an overly cash-constrained situation. You will want to make sure that no matter what type of loan program you decide on, you have enough money for a down payment, closing costs, and at least three months' worth of payments and expenses in reserve.

Reserves should be calculated based on covering your monthly payments and cost of living. Make sure you have enough set aside to cover at least a few months. Also factor in any repair or renovation work you might want to do. If buying a home could put you in a financially challenging situation, look for ways to find a lower price point, put less money down, or save more money before you begin your home search.

What is your financial discipline like?

Renting may make sense for some people on a purely financial model. If home prices are high and rents are lower, modeling it out might show that you are better off renting and investing the difference monthly.

The problem comes down to discipline. On paper it might make more economic sense—but are you *actually* going to save that extra money each month? Research says most people will not. One of the advantages of owning a home is that each time you make your monthly payment you are investing and saving by paying down your mortgage. In that sense, owning a home creates an automatic savings plan.

Before you start spending lots of time looking at homes, think carefully about the above issues to determine whether home buying is right for you. I believe that buying real estate is the surest way to build wealth for most people. It is the most common thread among the wealthy, and to say it again: Over 90% of millionaires built their wealth through real estate.

In the next couple of sections we will go over what to do and what to *avoid* when buying.

Step 2

Finance your home

Before you start to shop for your home, make sure you understand **how you will pay for the home and how that will affect your overall financial picture**.

Even if you think you will be paying cash for your home, you will at the very least want to understand your loan options, so **do not skip this section!**

In the past, lenders required buyers to put 20% down plus closing costs in order to get approved to purchase a home. In recent decades this has changed.

Loan products requiring far less money down have become available. Home buyers now have the option of taking out one bigger loan with additional mortgage insurance fees or getting a second, smaller loan.

In addition to having more options for their down payment, in recent decades home buyers have begun to have more options for the type of interest rate. Traditionally, the most common loans had a fixed rate for either 15 or 30 years. In the last few decades several new options emerged that usually took the form of some type of adjustable rate.

Adjustable Rate Mortgages (ARMs) typically have a lower interest rate for an initial fixed period and then adjust the interest rate based on the market as well as the terms and conditions of the loan.

Some lower down payment and adjustable rate loans make sense for many buyers today. Both loan features were abused and overused in the mid-2000s. Lenders offered loan products with extremely low initial interest rates with little or no down payment requirement. Some people in the industry offered these types of loans to home buyers who lacked the income or assets needed to safely take on the loan. As a result, the moment home values stopped going up at a double-digit pace and the first rate adjustment occurred, homeowners found themselves owing more than the home was worth and facing monthly payments that they could not make.

As a result of these past abuses, ARMs and loans requiring less than 20% down gained a bad reputation. However, for many home buyers, these types of loans can make a lot of financial sense if done safely and intelligently.

In the next part of this section we will go over the most common choices you will face while analyzing your loan options.

Down payment

Your down payment will have a lot of implications, including:

- The loan amount you qualify for
- Your overall monthly payment
- The interest rate

The more money you put down, the more you'll qualify for in loans—and the lower your monthly payment will be.

With more money down, the loan amount will decrease, *and* the interest rate on that amount will be lower. A loan's interest rate is based on several factors, one of which is the **loan-to-value ratio (LTV)**. LTV is a number indicating what percentage the loan is compared to the overall value of the home. So for a simple example, if you are putting down $20,000 on a $100,000 home, the loan will be $80,000 and the LTV will be 80 (80k/100k).

Loans that have a lower LTV/higher down payment are viewed by the lender as being less risky. Therefore, **rates are lower on loans that have a higher down payment**. This is true in most cases up to a down payment of 25%. Down payments higher than 25% affect the overall interest rate less.

What happens when you want to put less than 20% down?

When you put down less than 20%, you generally have two options. The first option is to take out one loan. Since the loan is greater than 80% of the purchase price, the lender will require mortgage insurance, which you pay monthly on behalf of the lender.

Mortgage insurance protects the lender in the event you default. This monthly payment will go away when the combination of paying down your principal and/or the rise in the value of your home increases your equity position to about 20%.

An alternative to your paying monthly for the mortgage insurance is to have the lender pay it up front. This is called **Lender-Paid Mortgage Insurance (LPMI)**. In exchange for this, your interest rate will be higher. This is usually a lower-cost option up front but more expensive in the long run. If the length of time you anticipate being in the home is short, LPMI might be a good option.

Your second option if you are putting down less than 20% is to take out a second loan. The first loan will typically, but not always, be around 80%. The second loan will be enough to make up the difference between your down payment and the first loan. The second loan typically has a higher rate and sometimes a shorter term. One advantage with this type of structure is that you have the option to pay off that second loan to reduce your overall payment. If you are expecting a lump sum of cash from a bonus, commission, inheritance, etc., you can pay off that second loan and get an overall lower payment.

Types of loan programs

The other big decision you will make with your mortgage is the loan type. In this section, we'll cover fixed rate loans, adjustable rate mortgages (ARMs), and special loan programs that require little or no down payment. **Start by deciding whether you want to get a fixed rate or an adjustable rate mortgage.**

Fixed rate mortgages have the same interest rate throughout the life of the loan. The most common terms are 15-year or 30-year loans. The rates on a 15-year loan are usually a little bit lower, but since the loan is paid off in half the time, the monthly payment is much higher.

Everyone has a different situation, but in comparison to the 15-year loan, I highly recommend the 30-year loan, since rates are near historic lows. In the future it is unlikely there will ever be an opportunity to borrow money as cheaply as current rates allow, so you might as well take the longest term possible in order to maximize your cash flow.

Adjustable rate mortgages (ARMs) have a fixed rate period after which the rate can adjust. All terms will be spelled out in the loan, but here is what you should look for:

- Initial interest rate
- Length of the initial term of the interest rate
- The index used to determine future rate adjustments
- The spread, or the amount above the index, that adjustments will be
- How long the periods are for each adjustment
- The maximum adjustments for each period and the life of the loan
- The minimum rate

An ARM will have an initial interest rate that is typically lower than that of a fixed rate mortgage. After an initial period, the rate will adjust. Common terms are 3, 5, 7,10, and 15 years. The adjustment is based on an index rate plus a spread. The index is typically some nationally tracked and published rate such as the one- or five-year LIBOR rate or the 10-year Treasury. The **spread** is the amount above the index that the adjustment will be.

For example, if the index is the five-year LIBOR and the spread is 2.5%, at the end of the initial term, if the five-year LIBOR is 3% the rate will become 5.5%. The adjustments can go up or down, but there usually is a floor that the rate cannot go below. Each adjustment will also have a term. Common time periods on the adjustments are one or five years. There are caps on how high each adjustment can be as well as a lifetime cap.

Despite the bad reputation that ARMs got in the mid-2000s, they can be a great option depending on the initial rate and term. You typically can save a lot of money up front in that initial term, compared to the 30-year rate, so **if you think you might move during the length of that term** or shortly after, an ARM might save you a lot of money.

Another more uncommon type of loan is the **interest-only** loan. In this type of loan, you only pay interest. At the end of the term you must pay the loan off or refinance. This was more common in the mid-2000s, but for some people might be a good option today.

Loan programs with low or no down payment

There are a few types of special lending programs that help buyers get homes with a very small down payment—or sometimes no down payment.

A **VA loan** is guaranteed by the U.S. Department of Veterans Affairs. Eligible active duty military members and veterans can get 100% financing on most homes. There used to be limits determined by area, but as of January 1st, 2020, those limits went away.

The VA charges a **funding fee**, which can be rolled into the loan. This funding fee is waived for veterans who have a disability rating with the VA. The amount of the funding fee varies depending on your down payment; your down payment reduces the funding fee.

VA loans also have other benefits. The program allows for much larger seller subsidies for buyers and a higher debt-to-income ratio for qualification. Another great benefit with VA loans is that they save money for borrowers every month because they **don't require private mortgage insurance**.

With the changes in 2020, there are no longer limits on the amount available for VA loans, but check for updates at our Home Buyer Secrets Resource Page at thehomebuyersecrets.com.

The **FHA (Federal Housing Administration) loan** is another special loan program popular for its low down payment options. An FHA loan is insured by the FHA. The FHA down payment and credit score requirements are much lower than those for conventional loans. **FHA loans are available to borrowers for as little as 3.5% down** if they have a credit score of 580 or better and 10% down for borrowers with credit scores between 500 and 580.

FHA loans require mortgage insurance, which is collected in two different ways. There is an up-front charge of 1.75% of the loan amount. There is also an annual premium that is paid monthly and varies between .45% to 1.05% of the loan amount based on loan size, length of the loan term, and LTV (loan-to-value) ratio.

FHA loan limits are set each year by the FHA. Limits vary by county. For the most up-to-date information on FHA loans and many other types of loans, make sure you have a great lender helping you and check our Home Buyer Secrets Resource Page at thehomebuyersecrets.com.

Keep in mind that some types of loans look strong to a seller. The strongest are conventional loans with 20% down. Loans with less money down look weaker to the seller. Loans with stronger financing terms generally will be more competitive and give you a better chance of negotiating a better price. For more on this topic, see the section on Crafting the Offer: 12 decisions that can save you money.

Choosing a lender

In addition to the type of loan you get and the size of your down payment, you'll need to choose a lender early in the process.

Loan interest rates are important, of course, but they're not the only thing to consider when choosing a lender. You should also consider a lender's reputation, speed, and level of service.

You should compare several lenders to evaluate your options. Do *not* wait until you have found your dream home to do this. A little time and effort up front will save you a lot of time and money, and will reduce the potential for headaches later in the process.

What should you look for in a lender up front?

Let the lender know what type of home you are looking for, including the area, home type, and price range. We'll talk more about these topics in the "Step 3: Search for homes" section later in this book.

Area, home type, and price range all determine the potential loan programs, rates, and terms you can use. You may find that your criteria shift after talking to lenders, and that is perfectly normal.

> **Home buying secret:** Prequalification and preapproval are *not* the same thing!

When you are doing your initial research up front, you should go through the process of getting **preapproved** for a loan. Getting preapproved means the lender verifies your credit, assets, and income up front, which is a little more in-depth than the traditional prequalification. Once you're preapproved, the lender should have a good idea of the types of loans you can get, the amount of cash you'll need to close, and what your monthly costs will be at various price ranges.

Some people will encourage you to just go through a quicker version of this called **prequalification**. The trouble with prequalification is that the lender will not actually verify credit, income, and assets. This could lead to surprises later, and the last thing you want is to go under contract on your dream home and then have a problem getting approved with your loan.

Almost every time I see an issue with a loan, the buyer could have saved hours of time and a lot of stress by simply taking a few minutes to get preapproved with the lender. If you go through this process early, you will find out if there are any issues documenting your criteria as a borrower. Things such as being self-employed, switching careers, not having your most recent tax filings done, and receiving large sums of money recently can cause issues, but **all of these issues are easier to deal with if the lender finds them early in the process.**

Many people ask about titles when buying a home, so let's address that now. The **title search** is something you pay for to make sure there is a clean chain of ownership of the home. You do not want some relative of the previous owner or someone else to come along claiming ownership of your home. The title search makes sure no one else would be able to make an ownership claim.

Title insurance protects you and the lender from such a claim. You are required by the lender to get title insurance protecting them up to the loan amount.

Owner's title insurance protects you up to the full amount of the home. Standard insurance protects you up to the amount of the purchase price, and enhanced insurance protects you on the future appreciation as well. While this will be done by the title company, the lender should be able to give you a good estimate of this cost.

You will want to **know the complete costs of your different loan option programs** and how much money you will need to close on your home. Usually you can expect this to be the down payment plus 2%–3% of the home's purchase price.

Going through this process with the lender should give you a good estimate of the programs, rates, and terms the lender can offer you, but it should also give you the chance to evaluate the lender using other criteria. Is the lender responsive? Do they provide good service? This is important, because in any market, speed can be an advantage that helps you get better financial terms on your home.

Here are some more questions you want to answer about your lender:

- How quickly can the lender close on the loans you are considering?
- How quickly can the lender get the appraisal done after you go under contract?
- What is their fallout rate (the percentage of loans that do not close)?
- How many loans do they make per month?
- Are they reviewed favorably online?

You want to make sure the lender you pick has the loan program you need and the ability to underwrite the loan ahead of time. You also want them to be competitive with their rate and costs.

You will want the lender to give you clear estimates of all the costs associated with taking out the loan and buying a home. Costs associated with the loan include points, origination charge, underwriting fees, appraisal, survey, prepaid reserves, etc. The estimate should also include costs *not* associated with the loan, such as taxes and title.

By the time you get through the financing step you should have a good understanding of the following:

- Which lender you are going to use
- Which loan types are options for you and the costs for each
- A range of how much money you have to put down
- How much your closing costs will be
- Any requirements or issues the lender needs you to resolve
- How long it will take the lender to complete each part of the process (appraisal, full loan approval, and closing)

Home buying secret

Be careful about shopping on interest rate alone. A lot of people do this and do not realize other fees are being tacked on to make up for the lower rate. And when it comes time to write the offer, you want a lender that can close quickly and deliver on their promises. **Service in the lending industry is just as important as interest rate**.

Search for homes

It's likely that you've already been window shopping for homes online or turning to look at homes you pass while driving that have "For Sale" signs posted, but your search is now about to begin in earnest.

Price, location, and type/features are the main decision points that will affect your home search. The interplay of these three decisions will determine how likely you will be to find a home.

We already talked a lot about financing in the previous section. After meeting with lenders, you should have a pretty good idea of the maximum price you'd be able to pay with your various loan options. You should also have an ideal price range. Begin your search with those numbers in mind.

The next big decision you will have to make is **location**. Location gives real estate its most unique characteristic. No location is the same as another, even on the same street. Start broad with this one and figure out the general area where you want to live (think county or city). Make sure the area has the community features you want and the overall feel that is attractive to you.

When shopping for a home, consider the proximity to restaurants, shops, parks, and other sites. People with school-aged children or plans to have children should also consider schools.

Home buying secret

You should examine the nearby schools even if you do not have children who will be attending. The quality of schools near a home is a strong enough factor to impact real estate values.

Once you have an idea of the general area you want to live in, you need to get more specific. Which part of the area would be best for you? What neighborhood? Do you want a cul-de-sac? Are you okay with living on a busier street? What about the view? All these questions will affect your home search.

The location will affect the *type* of homes that are available as well as the features. For example, if you want to live in an urban area, it is likely you will find more condos and townhomes. If you want an area with more space, you will likely find more single-family homes.

Let's briefly discuss the differences between these home types.

Condos

Although the word "condo" typically refers to homes in a single building or multi-building complex, **condominium** is a type of ownership structure. All condo owners belong to a condo association. They own their living space, and a percentage of the common spaces and elements. There is usually a monthly condo fee that covers services provided to the building, common insurance, and maintenance of the common elements. Typically, condos have a board of owners elected to serve on it. The board oversees the condo budget and the rules or bylaws. Usually when a person buys a condo they are given a legal time period to review the condo documents, financials, and rules. During this review period buyers can opt out of the contract.

Co-ops

A **cooperative (co-op)** resembles a condo: It's usually a group of homes in one building or a group of buildings. But co-ops have a completely different form of ownership. A co-op is a corporation. The corporation owns everything, including the individual homes. Co-op "homeowners" actually own stock in the corporation along with a perpetual lease to one specific home. Co-ops usually have higher monthly fees, but the fees cover a lot more expenses: property taxes, all utilities, insurance, and maintenance. The board on a co-op has a lot more power than the board at a condo or other type of homeowner association.

Townhomes

A townhome is a style of home, not a type of ownership. Townhomes are usually attached to other homes and have multiple levels. Most townhomes have **fee simple** ownership. Fee simple means you own everything from the ground to the roof, unlike condo ownership. Often townhomes are a part of a homeowner association (HOA). HOAs usually have a smaller fee that covers basic services and upkeep of sidewalks. The association is usually governed by a board elected by the homeowners and—like condos and co-ops—may have rules and regulations in a community. Unlike condos and co-ops, with fee simple ownership you are usually in charge of all maintenance related to your home.

Single-family detached homes

Single-family detached homes are typically sold with fee simple ownership. A single-family home will typically give you the most indoor and outdoor space as well as the most freedom when it comes to renovating, adding space, or making changes in general. Single-family homes come in many shapes, sizes, and styles: Colonial, Cape Cod, Rambler, Contemporary, and more.

Some single-family homes are in the area covered by a homeowner association, so you may be required to become a member. Single-family homes will also typically come with more maintenance items since they are bigger, and unlike condos or townhomes, single-family homes usually do not have a lot of maintenance items covered by the association. You can also expect to be responsible for the costs of all your utilities.

Home features

Another general consideration to make along with picking your home type is what **features** you want.
- How many bedrooms and bathrooms do you need?
- Are you okay with older features or do you want everything to be modern?
- What type of kitchen appliances do you want?
- What about other fixtures and countertops, cabinets, and flooring?
- What about amenities such as garage, pool, outdoor spaces, and anything else?

Our suggestion is to list the items that you "need to have" and separately list features that would be "nice to have." Get creative and take your time.

You should also do this with location: List all the features you "need to have" in an area and then list all the features that would be "nice to have." Once you have a good idea of price, location, and home type/features, you can move on to what we call the reality check analysis.

The reality check analysis

The **reality check analysis** is an exercise we go through with all our buyer clients. It's been so helpful for our buyers that we've gone on to teach the method to hundreds of real estate agents nationwide.

This reality check analysis is a simple exercise that lets you know whether your expectations are realistic, what to do if they are not, and how many homes that meet your criteria are likely to show up in your search. It is a data-driven way to take much of the guesswork out of your home search.

Begin by running a search of all the homes that have sold in the past 12 months that meet your criteria for price, location, and type/features. The only accurate way to do this is to access the **multiple listing service (MLS)**, so you will either need to acquire access to that or you'll need to work with a real estate agent.

Most agents do not start their buyer searches off this way, so if you are not working with an agent who has done this before, you might have to explain the process (or work with an agent who already knows how to do a reality check analysis).

So once you've entered your price range, location, type of home, and desired features, how many results did you get?

If you get no results it is likely that what you are looking for does not exist or turns over very rarely. Try searching back a few more years just to see if *any* homes at that price point meet your criteria.

If this second search also turns up no results, start changing your criteria and see what happens. What if you go up 5% on the price? What if you expand your location by a mile? What if you look for a smaller or older home?

Go on adjusting your criteria until you find records of homes sold that you would have been comfortable buying. If you had to adjust your criteria to find any sales, you want to note how *many* homes sold in the past year that met your adjusted criteria. Divide that number by 12 and it should give you the number of expected homes that will come on the market each month that meet your criteria.

If the number is less than one, you know you cannot be too picky when you see something you might want to buy. In low-turnover markets, you might need to be more willing to make repairs and renovations. You might have to go higher in price or take a location that is not perfect.

If there were multiple homes that sold per month meeting your criteria, you'll know you have more options to choose from.

Unless you take the time to do the reality check analysis up front, you won't know how flexible you can be in your search.

Step 4
Write an offer

When you've found a home you'd like to buy, it's time to present an offer to the seller.

In this section, you'll find two frameworks that Keri and I have developed for understanding factors and choices that will impact what price you decide to offer for the home.

The Four C's that determine home prices

The Four C's is a framework I developed early in my real estate career to teach clients the factors that affect home prices. This simple framework has now helped thousands of buyers understand ways to save money when negotiating for and purchasing a home.

The Four C's that determine price are:

- Contingencies
- Cash
- Closing Time
- Competition

Let's look at these in detail.

Contingencies

Contingencies are anything in a contract that makes the closing depend on something else. These tend to create risk for the seller. Here are a few common contingencies, in the order of riskiest to least risky:

- Home Sale
- Appraisal
- Financing
- Home Inspection
- HOA/Condo Review

If you want to get the best possible price or win during competitive offer situations, your best bet is to minimize these contingencies to the extent you are comfortable. Our team teaches clients up front in the initial meeting how to minimize contingencies while still protecting themselves.

Cash

The second C is **cash**.

This refers to the amount of money you put down for the deposit and the down payment. Bigger numbers give the seller more certainty. It lets them know you have more skin in the game and that you are qualified.

I've seen buyers get 3% or more off their home purchase just by going with a bigger-than-normal deposit.

Closing time

The third C is **closing time**. This refers to both the date you close on the house and the date you take possession. Sometimes the seller of a home will prefer time after closing to rent the home back from their buyer while they are preparing for their move. Often buyers can get thousands of dollars off the cost of their home purchase just by making the timing convenient to the seller. If you have the flexibility as a buyer, you might as well set a closing date and short rent-back period that work well for the seller in order to get the best financial terms. Being flexible on closing time costs you nothing, yet it can win you a better deal!

Competition

The fourth and final C is the **competition**. You will be operating within the constraints of supply and demand: In low-competition markets, prices will be lower. In high-competition markets, prices will be higher. This will vary according to the exact home type and location, so **even within the same zip code, the competition level can vary**.

Our team uses an off-market home program to help our clients make winning offers. When we can find homes for you *before* they go on the market, the competition is greatly reduced and the chances of winning a home increase.

If you can find homes before they go on the market you will save. We've added some examples of how we do this at the Home Buyer Secrets Resource Page, thehomebuyersecrets.com.

Crafting an offer: 12 decisions that can save you money

The Four C's give you an easy-to-remember framework for thinking about the factors that affect the price of a home. It works well because it is short, simplified, and memorable.

Keri created a more detailed and specific framework to prepare you for writing an offer on a home. This 12-decision framework takes you through *all* the key decisions you will need to make in that process.

These are impactful decisions that should never be left for the last minute. Knowing what these 12 decisions are at the start of your home search gives you the time you need to think about how best to use them.

Too many real estate agents—and therefore their clients—treat contracts as standard forms with standard recommendations on all terms and conditions. This thinking leads buyers to use terms and timelines in the contract that are based on industry standards from decades ago.

Writing offers the old-school way can cost you.

If you make your terms the same as the typical offer, that only leaves one thing to compete or negotiate on: **price**. To get a better price on your home, use the offer's terms to increase the seller's certainty that the deal will close. Reduce the friction of the sale by making things more convenient for the seller.

Let's examine all 12 decisions now, look at what the standard is, and then compare that to the better offer that you can make.

Decision 1: Closing date

The **closing date** is when you take ownership of the house. The typical time frames on closing date are 30–60 days from the date you and the seller go under contract.

Make your offer stand out by closing faster. Most sellers want the sale of their home to happen quickly, and your speed will increase their sense of certainty that you will get to closing if they take your offer. Unless the seller has a specific reason for not wanting to close fast, **shortening the closing date time frame will usually get you a better deal**.

So how fast can you close, and what do you need to think about beforehand?

A little-known secret is that you want to get fully approved by your lender early in the process. Verify that your lender can deliver on what they promise. (Note: If you are paying cash, the lender timeline does not apply; you will be limited only by the few days it takes for the title search on the home.)

Provided the lender can get you fully approved for the loan, you should have a clear idea of how quickly you can close. If the lender says they can close in 15 days and you make that your closing time frame, your offer will look better to the seller than one with a 30-day close.

Make sure you or your real estate agent verify up front when the seller would ideally like to close, make that happen, and you can get a better price.

Decision 2: Post-settlement occupancy

Some sellers want to rent the house back from the new buyer for a short period of time after the closing. They may need time to move, or they may need money from the closing of their existing home to purchase their next home.

Decide early on how flexible you can be with letting the seller rent the home back for a short period of time — usually two months at most. If you are getting a loan, the lender will usually require you to move into the house within 60 days of closing.

If you can show flexibility and **make the seller's relocation as easy as possible**, you will get better financial terms. Ask the seller or the seller's agent up front about an optimal closing date and move-out date. Know before you start your search what you're able to accommodate.

Decision 3: Earnest money deposit

You can leverage money that you would eventually put into your home anyway to get a better deal on your home. The **earnest money deposit (EMD)** is money you put in escrow with a third party when you agree upon a contract. The EMD is credited toward your closing costs and / or down payment.

The EMD protects the home seller in the *extremely* unlikely event that you default, break contract terms, and do not close on the home.

After closing thousands of homes, I have never seen a buyer lose his or her EMD—unless the default was intentional.

Here's how you get a better deal on a home with your EMD.

A lot of buyer agents tell their clients to put down 3%–5% for the EMD. But will that get you the best deal on the home?

When you put down a bigger EMD, you're sending the home seller the message that you are serious about closing on the home, because you have more skin in the game. With a larger EMD you're also showing the seller that you're a highly qualified buyer. The result: The seller has greater certainty that the deal will close. Peace of mind is worth a lot to home sellers. When you increase the seller's certainty, they'll be willing to decrease the price.

How much should you put down as an EMD?

This is your decision as the buyer, but I suggest looking at it this way: Any money you use for your down payment is going to be liquidated and put into the house within a few weeks to two months after going under contract.

For such a short period, most people would keep their money in a short-term holding place such as a bank. If your money is in a bank for two months, it will earn you nothing in interest.

But what could that money do for you if you use it for your EMD?

Let's do the math on a $500,000 home price as an example.

Let's say an old-school real estate agent told you to put down 5% for the EMD, so you're planning to put down $25,000. Now let's assume the down payment was going to be 20%, so that's $100,000.

What happens if you decide to put down a **20% EMD**, or $75,000 more? That would increase the seller's certainty of your seriousness. They're now looking at a $100,000 down payment instead of a $25,000 one.

With such a strong EMD, would the seller be more likely to give you a better deal on price? Of course.

What if that extra deposit got you just 1.5% off the price of the home? That would be an extra $7,500 for you. Your $75,000 just put you ahead by $7,500 in 30 days' time. That is a **10% return on your extra investment**

in just one month. If you annualized it, the internal rate of return would be well over 100%!

The size of your EMD is up to you, but I encourage you to think of it using the framework above. I've had several clients make their EMD the same size as the down payment. I even had one client **win a bidding war without being the highest price** because he put down an EMD that was bigger than the down payment and then got a refund at closing!

Decision 4: Lender and title company

This point is relatively easy: **Do your homework up front and pick a good lender**. A good lender will have a reputation of closing on time and with more certainty. When our buyers use lenders that have a good reputation, we can use that to help persuade the listing agent or seller. If the lender is good, often the listing agent will recognize the lender's name and that will work in the buyer's favor.

Make sure you use a good title company. In most areas, the buyer gets to choose. There are some sellers who have a preferred title company, especially when they're selling new construction homes. Often the seller will give you incentives to use the preferred title company. If that is the case, you will not only get the incentive but also make the transaction easier for the seller and therefore get a better deal.

If the seller does not have a strong preference here, go with a title company that has a great reputation. Your real estate agent should have a good recommendation for this.

Decision 5: Type of financing

The **type of financing** you get affects the strength of your offer. Not all loans have the same number of investors that buy them post-closing, which means some loans will present more certainty to the seller.

Conforming, conventional loans are the strongest offers, followed by non-conforming conventional loans, jumbo loans, and then FHA and VA loans.

For a refresher on the details of financing your home, review Step 2: Finance your home.

Home buying secret

I usually recommend using the strongest loan you can qualify for, even if you intend to switch to a different type of loan before the closing takes place. Most contracts allow for this with what is called an alternative financing clause, but if not, you can change the terms to allow it. As long as you close on time it is rarely an issue and by stating the strongest financing you qualify for in the initial offer you will get the best possible financial terms during negotiations.

Decision 6: Down payment

When it comes to **down payments**, bigger is better—at least in the eyes of the seller. A bigger down payment is going to make you look stronger as a buyer, and it makes getting qualified for a loan easier.

So the more money you can put down, the better. And yes, you can put a higher number in your offer (assuming you *could* afford that down payment size) and then switch to a smaller down payment later. If you close on time, it will not be a problem.

Decision 7: Seller subsidy

If you want the best deal, set the seller subsidy at zero and negotiate on price alone.

The **seller subsidy** is money the seller gives you at closing. If the seller gives you a subsidy, a common myth is that if you make up the difference in sales price, it is all the same. Wrong! A $500,000 offer is *not* the same as a $510,000 offer with $10,000 in seller subsidy because:

1. The seller will end up paying more in commission and taxes if the basis is $510,000.

2. Financing and appraisals are more difficult at a higher number.

So even though at first glance a $500,000 offer looks similar to a $510,000 offer with $10,000 in seller subsidy, the second deal actually pays the seller *less*, and the seller has more risk of appraisal or financing issues.

Set the seller subsidy at zero.

Decision 8: Financing contingency

The **financing contingency** gives you the right to get out of the contract if you cannot qualify for financing.

This contingency increases the seller's risk. There are two ways to decrease this risk and make your offer more competitive.

First, you can **shorten the length of the contingency**. A lot of agents use 21 days as the standard length. A good lender can get you approved and get your loan fully underwritten in half that time. Make sure you talk to your lender up front and have a very accurate sense of timing, and then shorten the contingency.

Second, you can **eliminate the financing contingency entirely**. The most competitive offers do not have a financial contingency. Many of our clients choose to go this route if they are in competitive situations or want to negotiate the best possible financial deal.

Decision 9: Appraisal contingency

The **appraisal contingency** resembles the financing contingency. In the event the appraisal comes in low or the lender requires certain repairs, an appraisal contingency gives you the right to renegotiate the contract and cancel if you and the seller do not reach an agreement. Most real estate agents will tell you to check the standard boxes here and ask for 21 days.

We have saved hundreds of clients money—sometimes over $50,000—by using alternatives to these old-school norms.

Here are three options for the appraisal contingency.

1. You can shorten the contingency's length. If you know your lender can turn the appraisal around in 7 days, why ask for 21?

2. You can limit the shortfall you will cover. For example, if the offer price is $500k, you can write an offer stating that you will not ask for the right to renegotiate if the property appraises for $490k.

3. You can decide not to include the contingency at all. This option will make the biggest impact on your offer.

Here are some important things to remember when making this decision: **Low appraisals do happen, but they are rare**—especially if you are using a solid lender. I see hundreds of transactions a year, and I can count the number of low appraisals per year on one hand.

Another thing to remember: A low appraisal is not the end of the world. If it does happen, you have options. The low appraisal only changes the value that the banks use to calculate their loan-to-value ratio.

If a bank is giving you a loan based on 20% down and an 80% loan, their rate and costs will be based on a **loan-to-value ratio (LTV)** of 80. At that ratio, for a

$500,000 home purchase, the bank would want $100,000 down and give you a loan of $400,000. If the appraisal came in $10,000 lower at $490,000, that would be the basis used to figure out the maximum loan. So you would multiply $490,000 by 0.80 to get a loan of $392,000 which would mean your down payment would have to be $8,000 higher: $108,000. Again, that's only if the appraisal comes in low, which is rare.

In that event, If you cannot get the seller to reduce the price of the home, your options would be to put down $8,000 more than you planned or restructure the loan and get one based on an LTV that is higher than 0.80. Neither option is really going to move the needle on whether it is a good long-term investment or a home you'll enjoy.

Of the thousands of buyers we have helped, **reducing or excluding appraisal contingencies has created far more benefits and savings** than negatives. Low appraisals are rare, and their impact is limited, so consider reducing or eliminating the appraisal contingency.

Decision 10: Home inspection

The **home inspection contingency** gives you the right to hire an inspector. If the inspector finds anything wrong with the home, this contingency then allows you to cancel the contract, negotiate repair items, and/or negotiate credits for repairs.

A lot of real estate agents with the old-school mentality just check in standard recommendations and timelines here, as they do with other contingencies.

So how do you protect yourself and reduce the risk to the seller so you can get the best possible deal?

The best way is to **do the inspection *before* you make the offer**. For reasons unknown to me, not all listing agents will recommend this to their sellers, but if the seller doesn't prohibit it, doing the inspection first will allow you to find out if there is anything wrong with the home and make the best possible offer to get the best possible financial terms.

If a pre-offer inspection is not allowed, you still have options.

Shorten the time. Many agents put a seven-day timeline on this contingency. You can almost always get the inspection done within days. If you or your agent have a relationship with a good inspector, and you notify them ahead of time, 24 hours is not out of the question.

Cover a certain amount of repair costs. Write in the contingency that you will cover the first $500 or $1,000 (or whatever number makes you comfortable) in repairs. This protects the seller from being nickel and dimed while protecting *you* if the inspector finds a major problem.

Make the inspection cancellation-only. This gives you the right to cancel the contract based on the results of the inspection without having the explicit right to negotiate for repairs.

> **Home buying secret**
>
> If your state has some sort of statutory review period such as a three-day condo document review, you can add a home inspection that matches that timeline and make the inspection informational only. You don't have the right to cancel under the home inspection, but if you find something alarming you can still cancel under the statutory review period.

All these options have helped make our buyers' offers more competitive, helped them win in bidding wars, and saved them thousands of dollars.

Decision 11: Home sale contingency

If you do not currently own a home, ignore Decision 11 and skip to Decision 12 below.

If you currently own a home, you need to determine whether it's necessary to sell it before you buy your next one.

The **home sale contingency** makes your contract to purchase contingent upon selling your existing home.

Avoid a home sale contingency at all costs, as it will crush your ability to negotiate with the seller of your next home.

There are two hurdles you need to clear. First, **you need enough money for the down payment** on your next home. For many buyers, that money is tied up in their existing home. Second, **you need to qualify for the existing mortgage *and* the new mortgage.** These requirements are tough for most people to meet.

Under these circumstances, how do you get the best deal?

One option is to ask your lender about a **bridge loan**. This is a loan that usually involves putting an additional lien on your existing home if you have enough equity. It is designed to be a shorter-term loan that allows you to close on your next home; the bridge loan will be replaced by a more permanent solution when your existing home sells. You usually will pay some extra points or fees on the bridge loan, but in our experience, it is worth it—you will usually save more than enough money to make up the difference by not including a home sale contingency in your offer.

Another option is to use a **home equity line** if you have enough equity.

If these options are not possible, you can put your home up for sale while searching for your new home. When you do get an offer, you will usually want to negotiate a 30-day or longer rent-back period as well as a longer contract-to-close period in order to maximize your chances of finding the right home. The risk with this approach is that you might have to move into short-term housing if the timing is not exactly right. We have had several clients choose this alternative, and while it can add short-term stress, it usually saves them money and works out fine in the end.

Another option is to find a real estate agent or team that offers a **guaranteed sale**. This is an option where your real estate agent gives you a guaranteed price, and if your home does not sell in time to buy your next home, your agent buys your home from you. We have offered this to buyers for years and bought dozens of homes through this program or similar programs.

A word of caution on guaranteed sale programs: **Ask about all terms and conditions** up front and ask how many times the real estate agent has followed through and purchased a client's home. Some real estate agents who advertise this program have never actually bought a client's home.

Our team has spent over $12 million backing up our guarantees.

You will get less money for your current home if you go with a guaranteed sale program, but you will also be able to make an offer on your next home that will save you money and give you peace of mind.

Decision 12: Purchase price

The final decision to make as a home buyer is the **purchase price**. This will depend on the exact home and the market at that moment in time.

Real estate is an inefficient market. There can and will be market variation month-to-month, week-to-week, and day-to-day. Because each home is unique and there is a limited supply on the market, it can be extremely hard to price homes with the accuracy buyers desire. This can be even harder in competitive markets when there are a lot of buyers and fewer sellers.

To start, look at comparable homes. You should look at homes that have sold and are under contract, current homes on the market, and homes that have been taken off the market without a sale.

Homes that have sold recently give you an accurate idea of what price the most recent buyers and sellers agreed upon, which is the definition of **market price**. Make sure you find similar homes in terms of age, location, and features. Adjust as needed based on whatever differences between comparable homes you find here.

Homes that are under contract can help you determine home price too, but since you do not know the closed price, a home under contract is *not* as helpful as a home that has already sold.

For more information on a home under contract, you could try to contact the buyer agent of a home to ask the exact price. Listing agents will almost never reveal that information, but a buyer agent might.

If all else fails, you should be able to **roughly guess the price of a home under contract** by the length of time that home was on the market. If the home was on the market for a few days or less, and you suspect there were multiple offers on the home, assume full price or more. If the home was on the market for more than a few weeks, compare it to the average home on the market for that time length in terms of sold price to list price.

Look at any listings recently withdrawn from the market. Withdrawn homes give you an idea of what price was too high for the market—the seller couldn't find buyers willing to pay. Markets can change quickly, though, so this isn't a perfect indicator.

Finally, homes currently on the market that are comparable to what you're searching for should give you an idea of what prices the seller's competitors are asking.

You should also evaluate how competitive the current buyer market is. How many months' supply of homes is on the market right now? Figure this out by dividing the number of homes currently on the market by the number of homes that went under contract in the past month. The resulting number is how many months it would take for all homes currently on the market to sell.

- A **buyer's market** will have more than six months' worth of inventory.

- A **seller's market** will have fewer than three months' worth of inventory.

- A **neutral market** will have between three and six months' worth of inventory.

When preparing to make an offer on a home, you should also look at **how long the home has been on the market**. If it is only a few days, don't expect to negotiate much in a seller's market. If the home has been up for sale longer than average for the market, you will have more negotiating power.

One final secret for making your offer is to **pick an exact number**. We have had great results with this. An offer of $539,957 appears to be more thought-out and therefore more serious than an offer of $540,000. If the other side in a negotiation thinks you put more thought behind the offer, they will consider it to be a more serious offer.

12a. Escalation up to:

In a competitive bidding war situation, you might need to use an **escalation clause**. An escalation clause says that you will increase your offer to a certain point if a competing offer is higher than yours.

How do you decide how high to go?

This is really a situation where you cannot rely on data as much as most people want. If other people are willing to go higher and you want the house but hold back because of market data, you will *not* be happy with the result. In bidding wars it is best to pick your **sleep number**—which is a better number than any real estate agent or market report can recommend to you. The "sleep number" is my name for the figure that would not keep you up at night if you lost the bidding war for the house.

Similar to our recommendations for offer price, I would use an exact number for the escalation clause.

12b. In increments of:

Another part of most escalation clauses is the increment that you will beat another offer by if it does not push you to the top of your bidding cap. This will depend on the price point.

I recommend you **set your escalation clause for at least 0.2%**. On a $500,000 home I would recommend at *least* $1,000.

More Ways to Win

Our team is constantly implementing more ways to help our buyers win in competitive situations. We are constantly finding new ways to help buyers save time and money, and reduce stress by negotiating better. To learn more of our latest techniques and get the latest updates, go to thehomebuyersecrets.com.

Step 5

Get under contract and close

So let's say the seller has accepted your offer and you have gone under contract. It's time to celebrate, right?

Not so fast.

You've passed an important milestone, but there is still a lot of work to do before closing. Here are four things to be aware of after you go under contract:

First, **make sure you immediately deliver your contract to the title company and lender**. Most contracts require this. Do *not* delay your delivery of the materials that the title company and lender need. When the title company or lender asks you for additional information or documentation, make sure you comply promptly. They want to help you, and the faster you respond, the less likely you are to have closing issues or delays.

Second, **make any required deposit** in a timely manner to comply with the contract.

Third, **schedule any necessary inspections quickly**. This might include home inspections, appraisals, and association document reviews. You want to get through inspections quickly to avoid being rushed by any contingency deadlines.

Fourth, **if issues come up, as a buyer you probably have more power than you think**. You can renegotiate terms or issues that come up during inspections no matter what the market is like. If you discover an issue with the house, or if your financing gets delayed for some reason (hopefully you selected the right lender to prevent that), in nearly all cases the seller will work with you. When you get down to the last 72 hours—no matter what type of market it is—the power tends to swing towards the buyer, as the seller really wants to get to closing. Finding another deal with a new buyer would reset the clock and waste a lot of the seller's time. Don't abuse this, but do realize that during the contract-to-close step, the power dynamic in any last-minute negotiations might shift in your favor.

Fifth, **try to stay calm** no matter what. The contract-to-close phase can be stressful. Getting things done early and having a positive attitude will help make closing as easy as possible.

Picking Your
Dream Team

If you've read this far, you've covered a lot of detailed information. You've decided whether buying a home is for you; you've chosen your desired location and home type; you've learned how to get financing; and you understand how to use the 4 C's and the 12 Decisions to get the best deal on your offer while still protecting yourself.

We have one more important item to cover, and that is **how to select the team** to help you find and buy your home.

Can you do all of this on your own? Absolutely, yes, you can.

Should you, though?

The overwhelming majority of buyers use a buyer's agent to represent them in their home purchase. A good real estate agent does all of this:

- Helps you select your home search criteria
- Educates you on the area
- Shows you homes
- Prepares your offer
- Guides you from ratified contract to closing

The above points are just for starters.

The **buyer agent fee** is almost always paid for by the seller. So for the small number of people who do not use a buyer agent, the question is: Why? Most people who attempt to go it alone think they can save money by going directly to the listing agent.

An unassisted buyer typically will ask the listing agent not to charge the seller full commission, or to rebate some or all of the buyer agent fee since there is no buyer agent involved.

There are at least three problems with this plan. First, the listing agent's contract with the seller typically allows the listing agent to keep the entire commission in this scenario, so the seller usually does not save money. The exception would be if the listing agent can actually be persuaded to change their existing agreement with the seller or choose to rebate money to the buyer. The listing agent has all the power in this scenario.

Second, some states simply do not allow rebates.

Third, even if the state does allow rebates, asking for these kinds of changes puts a listing agent in a pretty powerful position, especially since they represent the seller's best interests, not yours.

Here is an interesting data point on rebates in general. In our local area in the DMV, we have compared our statistics to a national real estate company. This company's main feature is rebating 1.5% (approximately half) of the total buyer commission back to the buyer in exchange for limited service. When we correct for home type, price range, and area, **our team typically gets our clients**

3% more off the list price than the competing national real estate company does for its clients. So clients of that service are paying 3% more and only getting 1.5% back. They're also receiving less service along the way.

Does that mean you always lose out if you go it alone or choose a limited service agency to give you a rebate back? No. There are some people that have the time, skill, and luck to pull it off. Some buyers can get it done, but what we have seen is that the vast majority of buyers who attempt to go it alone end up spending a lot more time and end up losing money.

We have given you a road map with a ton of secrets on how to attack the home buying process. If you take what we have given you and execute it flawlessly, you might be able to save money, but that is highly unlikely, especially when you factor in the value of your time.

The major reason people think they can do it better on their own is the lack of quality service in the industry. Now there are lots of good agents out there, but unfortunately there are even more bad agents. The bar to get a real estate license is low, but what it takes to succeed at a high level as a real estate agent is a lot higher.

Nearly 90% of real estate agents won't make it past five years in the industry. The average salary of an agent is usually less than $30,000, which means most agents don't have the money to invest in their training, marketing, and systems.

So if you are going to get professional help with your search (and almost everyone should), you need to figure out how to put together the best team and make sure you are hiring an agent in the top 10% or higher. Don't hire someone just because they are a friend, relative, or neighbor. Make sure you take the time to hire the best. If you are unsure what to look for, interview a few agents up front before you make a decision.

6 Things to know about a real estate agent before you hire one

1. **How much experience does the agent have?** The secret here is *not* to make this judgment by the number of years a person has spent in the industry. Many agents have had the same year of experience 20 times over. Instead, look for agents who have a lot of sales. The average real estate agent sells 12 or fewer homes per year. An agent or team completing 100 transactions per year acquires as much experience in *one* year as an average agent would take *eight years* to acquire. Our team sells several hundred homes per year.

2. **Is the agent going it alone?** Just like it's usually not the best idea for a home buyer to go it alone, the same is true with a real estate agent. Look for teams or agents that have hired multiple supporting players. If your agent works alone and a great property comes up, you might not be able to act fast enough if that solo agent is on vacation, sick, or at another appointment. No buyer should lose out on their

dream home just because their agent is busy; that's why we've built our team to provide coverage no matter what. We have over 60 specialized team members dedicated to serving our clients.

3. **Can the agent find you homes off-market?** You want an agent who will do more for you than just set up an MLS search. You want an agent who knows how to find you homes *before* they go on the market. To find these off-market homes, an agent must have great marketing systems, the ability to prospect, and the drive to get the job done. When you are interviewing agents, ask them how many homes they have helped people buy off-market. Off-market homes are important even in a buyer's market because they will give you more options. Our team sells nearly *one third* of our homes off-market.

4. **What kind of reviews does the agent have?** Don't just listen to agents talk about their track records. See for yourself what client testimonials and reviews they have online. Zillow, Yelp, and Google are all third-party sites where you can find reviews of real estate agents and teams. Feel free to look up The Keri Shull Team while you're at it—we have *hundreds* of five-star reviews.

5. **What kind of relationships does the agent have with other vendors?** A successful real estate transaction usually involves an entire team of experts: the real estate agent, lender, title company,

inspector, contractors, and more. Ask agents you are interviewing what relationships they have with these types of service providers. Real estate agents who do more transactions will usually have better vendor relationships, which can play a critical role in a successful home buying experience.

6. **What does the agent do to invest in themselves?** You don't want a real estate agent who is not investing in training or business coaching. You want an agent who is dedicated to learning and continually growing. Keri and I dedicate about 10% of our time each year and spend tens of thousands of dollars to get business coaching from the top trainers and consultants in the world. It is well worth it and we always bring back more value that we can deliver to our clients.

We also invest time in training our team members. Our training programs have been so successful that we now train hundreds of real estate agents across the world who take part in our membership programs, courses, and live events.

Conclusion

We understand that the home buying process can be stressful, whether you're buying for the first time or trying to handle the sale of your current home with the purchase of your next one.

Our goal is to make the process easier for you. To reach that goal, we use the experience we have gained helping thousands of buyers. We train and learn from real estate agents on our own team and all over the world. We want to save you time and money while making the process stress-free.

If we help just one person do that through this book, the hours of writing, editing, designing, and publishing will be worth it.

If you are buying a home in the DC, MD, or VA area, we can tell you with 100% certainty that there is no other team in this area that helps as many buyers as we do. We would love to help you buy a home, and if you need to sell, we can help you with that as well.

If you go to www.hirethebestintheDMV.com, you'll find a FREE, frequently updated resource pack you can download.

If you are looking for a home anywhere else, we can help you find the best real estate agent in your target area. We coach real estate agents all over the world.

Go to www.hirethebestagentanywhere.com to learn how we can get you the best agent.

Thank you again for reading. We wish you the best in your home buying journey.

Notes

Notes

Notes

Made in the USA
Middletown, DE
06 January 2021